Get Ready! Get Real! Get Financial Freedom!

A Simple Blueprint for Building and Sustaining Financial Freedom

By

JEFFREY A. JOHNSON SR & TIM WHITE III

Printed in the United States of America

First Printing, 2020

ISBN 978-1-7343118-0-8

Opes Publishing Co.
Atlanta, GA

www.opespublishing.com

Dedication

Before you speak, listen. Before you write, think. Before you spend, earn. Before you invest, investigate. Before you criticize, wait. Before you pray, forgive. Before you quit, try. Before you retire, save. Before you die, give.

—William A. Ward

Jesus said twenty times more about money than he did about the kingdom, prayer, or fasting.

—Vernon Johns

Contents

Foreword

Throughout the Book of Proverbs, God's people are encouraged to get wisdom and understanding in order to succeed in life. While these proverbs were written thousands of years ago, the principles still hold true today. Despite what society deems as success, in order to truly be free, we must seek to understand biblical principles and learn how to apply them to every aspect of our personal lives, including our finances. Get Ready! Get Real! Get Financial Freedom! is a much-needed tool that guides readers along the path of financial freedom using the Word of God as its foundation. While the steps to achieving financial peace may be simple, the authors Jeffrey Johnson and Tim White admit that it isn't easy. Yet, for those who are willing to commit to a few basic changes, the promise of a more abundant life can be theirs!

John K. Jenkins Sr.

Senior Pastor
First Baptist Church of Glenarden, Maryland

Introduction

It Is Simple!

There is no greatness where there is not simplicity, goodness, and truth.
—Leo Tolstoy

And my God shall supply all your need according to His riches in glory by Christ Jesus.
(Philippians 4:19)

If you are reading this book in search of a complex, sophisticated, Six Sigma, or NASA- generated mathematical approach to building financial freedom, this book may not be for you. However, if a simple, realistic, and practical approach to building and sustaining financial freedom is what you desire, don't stop reading! You can have as much financial freedom and success as you desire and stay that way for life.

In fact, growing and sustaining financial freedom is astonishingly simple. What is meant by the word "simple"? Famed abstract artist Hans Hofmann defined it well: "The ability to simplify means to eliminate the unnecessary so that the necessary may speak."

Allowing the necessary to speak or understanding what is important involves the ability to clear away the clutter in our minds and lives. This extra clutter often causes doubt, stagnation, and indecision, along with an endless cycle of the same old lifestyle with zero progression. When we simplify our lives, it creates the clarity needed to see how we can achieve financial success and the success in life we so desire.

We often envy those who are enjoying financial freedom and abundance. Somehow, they have found a pool of unlimited time and resources. The serial entrepreneur with all the successful start-ups seems to have all the time in the world. The visionary movie director from Hollywood turns out one masterpiece after another. The prolific and highly respected writer pens countless successful books with apparently no effort. How do they do it? What is the secret that makes them so productive?

Time is the great equalizer. No one can claim anyone has more time than you do. We all have the same twenty-four hours each day. No matter how talented you are or how successful you have become, twenty-four hours is all there is. So, how do the super-productive people do it?

Think about the last time you watched a movie on Netflix without a specific movie in mind. You most likely spent a tremendous amount of time scrolling up and down before deciding. Some of you may even have closed down Netflix entirely without having watched anything. Remember the last trip to a new restaurant without knowing what you wanted to eat? Shifting through the mounds of choices may have annoyed your hunger away.

Even scrolling through Apple News, LinkedIn, Snapchat, Instagram, or Facebook creates thousands of little choices we need to make: what to read, what to like, what to disagree with, and what to pay attention to. Why does this happen to us all? Too many choices clamor for our attention, overwhelming our minds. Making a decision is taxing and leaves us fearful that we might be missing out if we make the wrong one. We end up in this state of non-decision, wishing that some outside force would intervene and make the decision for us.

What's the secret of successful people? They learn how to simplify the decisions in their lives by focusing on the few they make instead of becoming mentally paralyzed by the distractions of too many. Colossians 3:2 exhorts us to "set [our] mind[s] on things above, not on things on the earth." When we simplify our mind's focus, the result is sharper clarity.

Exercising the muscles in our body drains energy, and the same is true when we use our brains. For this reason, successful people who make hundreds, if not thousands, of decisions every day try to reduce the number of trivial decisions they have to make in order to reserve energy and increase their productivity.

Have you ever noticed that Mark Zuckerberg and Steve Jobs always wear the same type of clothes? They are constantly bombarded with decisions they have to make, both big and small. For them, what to wear to the office is not one of those choices. They save their mental energy for more important decisions.

How much time do you waste getting ready for work, a date, or simply leaving your house, only to realize that once you finally get out, your patience is thin and energy low? This combination does not usually result in a great day or evening. Why not save your energy and increase your productivity by simply making fewer choices? Cut out the unnecessary, as Hofmann stated in the opening quote. Don't allow decision fatigue to creep into all aspects of your life.

Although having several choices is often what we want, it is not always healthy for us. The late pastor A. Louis Patterson, Jr.

once stated, "What keeps you from getting what you want most is what you want."

Psychologist Barry Schwartz coined the phrase "paradox of choice" to describe his consistent research findings about indecision. Schwartz suggest that even though an increase of choices allows us to achieve objectively better results, it also leads to greater anxiety, indecision, paralysis, and dissatisfaction.

Instead of empowering us to make better choices, our almost unlimited access to information often leads to a greater fear of making the wrong decision, which can cause us to spin our wheels in a seemingly inescapable purgatory of analysis paralysis—all while getting nowhere on our important tasks and goals.

If you simplify or reduce the overall amount of decisions you make, you can be more productive, efficient, and effective regarding the important decisions you *do* make. Individuals who are financially free know and use the power of simplicity to build and sustain financial success.

A practical way to accomplish this is by utilizing the Warren Buffett two-list approach. Make a list of the top twenty-five goals you want to achieve, in order of priority. Draw a line underneath the fifth priority. Warren states, "Everything below #5 you should avoid at all costs. You should work towards not working on any of them." The "Top 25" list effectively becomes two lists—"work" and "avoid." If you have achieved 100 percent of your work list, then that's the only time to re-open your other list. Stop and take the time now to make your list!

Bottom line: Building and sustaining financial freedom starts with simplicity. Learn how to simplify your life by not making less non-important decisions that drain your mental energy. Do so and you will increase your productivity, which will lead to success in reaching your goals.

Simplicity is an incredibly powerful universal tool for building success in life. No matter whether it involves building finances, faith, successful relationships, or profitable companies, simplicity works!

Herbert David Kelleher was a young Texas lawyer before leaving his firm to found Southwest Airlines in the sixties with this one *simple* goal: providing low-cost transportation from Houston, Dallas, and San Antonio. He not only succeeded, but as of July 2008, Southwest Airlines has been profitable for thirty-three consecutive years, and for the last 127 consecutive quarters, it has paid a dividend to its shareholders. Its balance sheet, with about three billion dollars in cash on hand and six hundred million in available credit, is now the envy of a fuel price-ravaged industry. What did Kelleher do at Southwest that no one else in the airline industry was doing?

He kept his business simple and consistent, which drove costs down, maximized productive assets, and helped manage customer expectations. Kelleher did this with a one-plane- fits-all model. Unlike all other carriers and their commuter surrogates, which operate all manner of regional jets and turboprops, as well as narrow-body and wide-body aircraft, Southwest utilizes just one plane type, the Boeing 737 series. This saves Southwest millions in maintenance costs—spare-parts inventories, mechanic training, pilot training, and other airline inventory issues. Simplicity works!

We often believe the erroneous ideology that success, financial freedom, and greatness is only for the chosen few, and it is this impossible task to achieve. For some reason we tend to believe the greatness achieved and personified by others is a luxury only given to the chosen few among us. Not so! It is available to us all. I love the way Will Smith describes greatness: "Greatness is not this wonderful, esoteric, elusive, God-like feature that only the special among us will ever taste. It's something that truly exists in us all."

Once you have completed reading this book, my goal is to ensure you truly believe you can be as financially successful as you want and have the blueprint to carry it out. Every reader should not just be excited but truly believe that it can happen—and the strategy is simple!

Why can you be confident in one day being prosperous? First of all, Philippians 4:13 tells us, "I can do all things through Christ who gives me strength." Also, there are 1,700 new millionaires every day, according to Ben Steverman of Bloomberg. Credit Suisse's new Global Wealth Report 2017 states that there are now thirty-six million millionaires in the world. In 2013, the Credit Suisse published a report suggesting that 20 percent of the world's population could be millionaires within two generations. In other words, sometime before 2073 (as of the report's writing) there could be a billion millionaires walking the earth. There is a real possibility you can be one of them.

Financially successful individuals are not just wealthy heirs, entrepreneurs, or even high- powered executives. In fact, the largest percentage of millionaires based on career category was educators and managers, according to the Spectrum Group's report. These are everyday people just like you! No matter who you are or where you are financially, as you read this understand that being successful and living the life God desires for you and you want to live can be simple.

There is a human tendency to believe that major success must be complicated. A study shows that over 70 percent of Americans do not believe they can ever become financially free. As a result, many have resigned themselves to watching others become successful. They are okay with not making it on their own, essentially handing over their financial future to another. If you are reading this book, I assume you refuse to settle for watching others become financially successful while you sit on the sidelines. This book is designed to be your user manual providing resources with the help of the Lord for building and sustaining financial freedom.

> *Greatness is not this wonderful, esoteric, elusive, God-like feature that only the special among us will ever taste. It's something that truly exists in us all.* –Will Smith

So, let us begin!

Chapter 1

Breaking the Holding Pattern

*If you think you can or you think you can't
you're right!*

—Henry Ford

Many of us awaken each morning with a deep desire for something more. We know deep inside the life we are living is not all that life has for us. Despite knowing this, we are still guilty of waking up and repeating the same cycle. Like a hamster on the wheel in a cage, many of us run hard but make no forward progress. It's just as if we're human robots programmed for monotony and mediocrity.

Perhaps during your daily routine you work out, or not. Or maybe you head to work hating the traffic, the car you are driving, and the feeling you get knowing you'll have to walk into your workplace. You constantly think about how much you dread your job and/or your boss. Maybe you just want a vacation but can't afford it, or your boss will not give you the time needed to take one. Perhaps you just want the best for your children but can't afford the schools that will give them the best start. Even those of you who are entrepreneurs enjoy what you do but have not yet found a way to move forward. So, you keep doing the same things—over and over. Around and around you go.

Some of you insist, "At least I am not going backwards." However, many would argue that if you are staying the same, you are essentially going backwards. There is really no such thing as staying the same; either you're growing or regressing. Many of you have literally been mentally programmed to endlessly go around in circles without making any real progress. You're busy but not productive. You're moving frequently, but you're not going anywhere. Ultimately, you have found yourself stuck in a holding pattern, and the frustration and mental anguish of your ongoing inertia is often indescribable. You live for the short weekend, while five out of seven days a week you feel trapped in despair. How do you break this cycle? You must first identify what a holding pattern is.

While studying for my private pilot license, I learned some great lessons applicable to life. In aviation, holding (or flying a hold) is a maneuver designed to delay an aircraft already in flight while keeping it within a specified airspace. If you fly often, you may have experienced the inconvenience of being placed in a holding pattern during a flight.

According to the Flight Safety Foundation, "Holding patterns are flown as a delaying tactic, be it for Air Traffic Control (ATC) requirements such as airspace saturation or approach delays, the termination of a missed approach procedure to be flown while coordinating further clearance, at pilot request to allow time for completion of abnormal or emergency checklist procedures, or at any other time that a delay in flight progress is required." Bottom line: A flight only enters a holding pattern when something within the original flight plan has gone wrong.

Perhaps ATC couldn't clear the plane because of air traffic congestion or other factors beyond the pilot's control in flight. Or, a problem with the landing equipment needed to be resolved before the pilot attempted to land. He might have even attempted to land, but the attempt failed, forcing him to circle before he tried again. Whatever the issue, the plane is stuck in a circling pattern, not able to reach the desired destination.

Does this sound familiar? Are you stuck in the same old rut? Have you tried and failed to land your finances in a great place? Are you failing to reach your potential? You end up making the same or less money each year, so you can't make enough to save or get ahead. You may have dreamed of starting your own business or simply enjoying financial freedom, when actually you find yourself endlessly going around in circles about everything in your life. Being stuck in a holding pattern seriously feels like the worst place ever! Yet, if you find yourself in this place, that's good news because you are now so tired of being stuck there that you desire to do something about it.

There is no better time than now! Be audacious and throw the switch in your mind to change things for the better forever. You may ask, "How? What do I do?" It's simple, remember! Don't overcomplicate it.

Sigmund Freud, an Austrian neurologist and the founder of psychoanalysis, a clinical method for treating psychopathology through dialogue between a patient and analyst, once said that the first step toward solving a problem is the realization you have one in the first place. If you are honest with yourself, it's hard to end the charade and admit you have an issue that is keeping you stuck in the same pattern. You must make the personal decision to resolve it. You must be ready to go somewhere different and better. Indeed, that decision to break your holding pattern and change your financial situation must be a top priority in your life.

One of the most profound statements I've ever heard helps us understand how we can break our holding patterns in a practical way. It comes from the most unlikely source, and best of all, it's magnificently simple! In the 2019 Disney movie *Christopher Robin*, Winnie the Pooh says, "I always get where I'm going by walking away from where I've been."

> *"I always get where I'm going by walking away from where I've been."* –Winnie the Pooh

It's time to walk away from the same old circles, break the patterns, and build a new financially free life. This book will serve as your Air Traffic Controller (ATC), the guide to help you navigate to your new destination. By following the instructions of the ATC, you can break the holding pattern that has held you in its grip for years.

One lesson my flight instructor taught me is forever ingrained in my mind. He simply said, "It is critical to always remember one thing: *You are the pilot in command!*" Simply stated, all final decisions and actions are always yours to make. This plane (your life) only goes where and when you tell it to go. If you end up anywhere else, it is your responsibility as the pilot in command.

God has given us the ability to make our lives successful. Specifically, Deuteronomy 8:18 says that He gives us the power to gain wealth. To accomplish this goal, we must first seek God's counsel and then make our decisions as the pilot in command.

Even though Air Traffic Control (your parents, mentors, friends, and siblings) usually has your best interests in mind, ATC is not aware of the immediate situations in your life, which is very important. People can often see the weather, perhaps have gone down similar paths, and in most cases, they have your best interests in mind. However, no one but you knows what's going on in the cockpit real time. So, when making decisions, you must keep that in mind.

You are the captain! Information from others is great and needed sometimes, but you are the one best fit to take all that input and access it on the backdrop of what is going on real time in your cockpit. ATC is safe in the tower giving you the best information they have as they look at your life from the outside in. You can use the advice they give you, but remember that you are the pilot in command. Sometimes you have to tell ATC what's best for you.

Now let's go one step further by truly admitting to ourselves that we have been in a holding pattern regarding money. Our finances are not where they should be. Take the time to do an honest reflection and then write down at least ten activities you have been or are now doing that have caused you to get stuck. Why can't you land or take off? Are you spending more than you make? Are you procrastinating or not taking accountability for your life? Is your credit card debt getting larger? Are you honest with yourself? Is your ego or pride holding you back?

It is important that you're very specific when generating this list. If you're going to break the holding pattern, you have to know what's holding you. If you need help, find someone in your life whom you can trust to be honest with you. If what they share about you only makes you a little uncomfortable or even perhaps slightly offended, either they are probably not telling you the truth, or you are not sharing the whole story with them. Growth hurts, so if this written process of admitting your shortcomings is not uncomfortable, you're not being honest and you will stay stuck. If you cheat while building this list, you only cheat yourself and no one else is to blame.

These are samples of items that could be on your list:

I shop too often for things I really don't need.	I never take any accountability for anything, especially anything that goes wrong.
I try to impress people, so I pay for everyone a lot.	I don't believe I can actually be rich and successful.
I travel beyond my means.	I'm scared of being rich and successful.
I typically spend the same amount or more that I make each month.	I am acting like someone else and spending based on what I believe they do.
I don't budget, so I don't know how much I actually spend.	I spend time focused on other people's lives and not my own.
My credit card debt and balance is high, and I only pay my minimum each month.	I'm not really kind to people, and I'm not a great team player.

My pride causes me to buy things to impress people, such as cars, clothes, and shoes—as well as additional things I can't afford.	I don't save at all.
I eat out way too much! I don't know how to say no to friends.	I waste a lot of time on social media.
I procrastinate on pretty much everything.	I am blaming everyone else a lot, even when I know I'm wrong.
I am notorious for not following through on commitments I make to myself and others.	I watch a lot of non-educational TV (Netflix, cable, YouTube).

Once you have completed your personal list, write STOP DOING IMMEDIATELY in large letters at the top. Print out the list and put it in places you can't avoid, such as your phone and computer screensavers. Read it multiple times every day. Constantly remind yourself that you are not getting caught in any more holding patterns. Refuse to be broke. Write on a piece of paper, "I refuse to be poor, broke, or financially dependent anymore! I will not quit until I succeed. I refuse to settle for anything less than financial independence and abundance."

Remember, as you think in your heart, so are you. If any item on your list falls outside of the will of God, pray and ask the Lord to forgive you because negative consequences always follow disobedience to God. First John 1:9 says, "If we confess our sins, He is faithful and just to forgive us *our* sins and to cleanse us from all unrighteousness."

At this point in the book, you may be thinking to yourself that we have not discussed much about financial principles. You are somewhat correct. However, it is for a very important reason: you have to get ready first! What is meant by the phrase, "get ready"? Part of being ready involves being mentally prepared. If you are not mentally prepared first, you can have all the financial tools in the world and still be stuck. To do this kind of preparation, you must recognize and nurture the power of your mind.

If you can't control your mind, you can't control your finances. This chapter, as well as the next two, will help you start stretching and strengthening your mind for the new level you are heading. You can't go anywhere without your mind being there as well, so your mind must be ready.

It is vital for you to prepare and program your mind for building and sustaining financial freedom. A healthy human mind is inarguably one of the most inconceivably powerful tools at your disposal, no matter what your background, race, gender, or financial status may be. In fact, the only consistent, dependable source of power available to any human being is the power of his or her own thoughts. Everything in the world that is not naturally formed from the earth originated from someone's imagination. How incredible is that!

This is why shaping and training your mind is vital to creating the life you want to have. Your mind holds all that you believe about yourself, which is what ultimately becomes your reality. Having the right frame of mind and belief in oneself is essential to building and sustaining wealth. You have to believe in yourself and constantly replay that which you believe about yourself in your mind on a daily basis.

Hollywood films have often portrayed lions as the "kings of the jungle." (For the sake of accuracy, though, lions don't actually live in jungles at all.) Actually, this title has been ascribed to lions regarding their status at the top of the animal kingdom or animal food chain. Interestingly, however, lions are really not the largest, strongest, fastest, heaviest, and smartest animals of all. Yet, they are still considered to be kings. Have you ever wondered why that is? If it is not their physical prowess that commands the respect of other smarter, larger, faster and stronger animals, what is it? How are lions able to make a feast out of animals tremendously larger and stronger than they are?

It's all due to the lions' attitude that they continually display. Lions don't fear any other animal. When it comes to protecting their pride or hunting for food, their mindset supersedes all of their shortcomings. They simply don't focus on what they don't have. Instead, they use all the strengths they do have in order to get what they want to have. The superior intelligence, size, speed, or power of the opposition is irrelevant and of no concern to the lion.

Dr. Henry Cloud helps us better understand this concept. He states, "Your attitude is more important than the facts. Any fact facing us, however difficult, even seemingly hopeless, is not as important as our attitude toward that fact."

Never allow the facts of your current situation to define and confine you. Neither should you ever allow labels to limit you. Some people will seek to label you with the intent to limit you. Your job is not to allow them to put limitations on your life.

What can we learn from the attitude adopted by lions that will help us develop a healthy mindset so we can build our financial freedom, as well as allow us to see ourselves the way God does?

- Belief in yourself is paramount to your success.
- The facts of your circumstances, whatever they are (especially those regarding anything in opposition to your goals) are not as important as your attitude toward those facts.
- Stop spending time focusing on what you don't have and start using what you do have to build what you want to have!

This is why a lion, when seeing an elephant, thinks, *It's dinner time.* When you see an elephant of a problem or opportunity, what do you tell yourself? It's time you start programming your mind to say, "Dinner time!" You must firmly believe you can overcome any problem, despite any personal shortcomings or opposition of any kind.

If you are going to break the holding pattern, you must—just as the lion does—believe you can. Be a lion in your life, especially in your finances. Once you believe you can, then simply make the decision to break out and never go back. Remember, you are always the pilot in command. ATC may not clear you to land at the original destination, but you can always break out of the holding pattern and choose a new destination. Making that decision is always up to you. If by chance you are tired of circling around in life, decide now to break the holding pattern. My advice is not to wait until you run out of fuel, because that will cause you to crash and burn.

You must have the courage to believe in the vision God has given you. Visualization is the ability to be able to see what you desire before you actually receive it. You must see it before you see it, if you are ever going to see it. You must see it to become it. You must behold it before you become it. The greatest athletes from the past and present, such as Tiger Woods and Serena Williams, have visualized the victory before actually achieving it.

In summary, how do you break the holding pattern?

1. **Admit it!** Recognize the reality that you are stuck and actually in a holding pattern. Find out how you got there, and immediately stop doing those things forever.
2. **Believe it!** Believe you can break the pattern by believing in yourself and constantly strengthening that belief in your mind. See the vision of yourself as financially free. Be a lion!
3. **Break it!** Walk away and never go back. Remember, you're the pilot in command of your life. You have to recognize honestly what got you in that pattern and what can keep you out. Continually practice the positive habits and tools used to break it, and vigilantly watch for the bad habits that cause you to enter the holding pattern.

Chapter 2
Understanding Why Money Matters

Money, whether you have it or not, whether you want it or not, whether you like it or not, will try to define your days. Our task as human beings is not to let it.
—Phil Knight, Nike Co-founder
and Chairman Emeritus

Understanding why money matters is crucial to building and sustaining financial freedom. If you understand why money matters, the money you have will never have you. You will always be in control and not allow it to ever define you, as Phil Knight suggests.

It is also important to understand that even though money does matter, in some cases it does not work best for accomplishing your goals. In this chapter we will explore popular misconceptions about money and ultimately understand why money matters.

Our conception of money shapes and molds our actions in regard to our finances. Just as the beliefs you hold about yourself direct your actions in life, so also your beliefs and understanding about money shape and direct the actions you take with your finances. Some beliefs about money are shaped in experiences from childhood as well as the young adult years. However, some scholars maintain that decisions and actions made in adulthood stem from experiences in adulthood.

According to journalist Paul Wanaye Wamimbi, in his article regarding how culture and values shape our lives, "Beliefs come from real experiences, but often we forget that the original experience is not the same as what is happening in life now." These experiences, when not retooled for the reality of our current individual lives, can be damaging to our finances because of what they cause us to believe about money.

Think about what you saw, heard, and witnessed regarding money as a child or young adult. Take a moment to sincerely think about how your parents, grandparents, or the individuals you admired handled money. In most cases you will notice a striking resemblance to the way you handle money. For some of you growing up, money came into the family bank account and went out in a short time frame. Thus, you believe money must go as soon as it comes. "Spend, spend, spend" is your programmed understanding. For others of you, money always triggers arguments because you often heard your parents or those close to you argue regarding money.

For some of you, money is evil because it is always at the center of your worst memories and fears. Perhaps you have always heard a loved one say money is not more important than love. So today you devalue money and throw it away, both subconsciously and physically in pursuit of more love. You may also believe money represents systemic racism, sexism, and classism, which has caused you to be cynical about those possessing financial freedom or having it for yourself.

Money also can signify insecurity that readily surfaces because of the shame it caused you in the past from not having enough. So, you never talk about it. As a result, you never get the guidance you really need. This mindset is prevalent in many cultures. Many don't openly discuss money with anyone, especially their children. Unknowingly, someone in your past handicapped your personal financial growth by not talking about money or shaping positive habits in you regarding money. Nevertheless, it is your responsibility to do something about it now!

Our mental programming regarding money typically comes from a source uneducated about finances. We unknowingly repeat cycles that are subconsciously programmed in us from childhood. No one taught our parents or their parents, and as a result, we have repeated the same cycle. To help end this vicious cycle, let us begin by flushing out the misconceptions about money and share the basics of why money matters.

Let's take a look at a few of the more prevalent false ideologies regarding money.

- Love is more important than money.
- Money is evil.
- Money changes people.
- It takes money to make money.
- The rich get richer and the poor get poorer.
- I can't live a balanced life if I want to make a lot of money.
- My financial success depends on the job market and the economy.
- To make money, I must take *huge* risks.
- Money is the measure of my success and/or worth.
- Most wealthy people are like Ebenezer Scrooge—selfish penny-pinchers.
- In climbing the ladder of success, you have to step on others on the way up.
- You have to be in certain professions to make a lot of money.

While often repeated, none of these statements is accurate. They only lead us to believe that we should not be financially free. We will not touch on them all; however, we will speak on the first three.

The misconception that money is not more important than love is repeated frequently in our society. Most would agree they have encountered this myth at least once, most likely by reading it in a book or hearing someone talk about it. T. Harvey Elker, in his book *Secrets of a Millionaire's Mind*, best explains why this statement is not accurate. He tells a story that occurred during one of his speaking engagements. As he was speaking, a person stood up in the crowd and shouted, "Money is not more important than love." Elker responded to this individual by saying, "You're broke, aren't you?" This individual looked down and slowly responded with much embarrassment, "Yes, yes, I actually am."

In his book, Elker continues by clarifying this often misunderstood notion. He states that "love is not more important than money, but money is also not more important than love." As a matter of fact, Elker elaborates that "love is very important where it works and very unimportant where it does not. Money is very important where it works and very unimportant where it does not."

To make this real for you, if you tried to pay your mortgage, light bill, or car note with love, you would find out in short order that love is very unimportant to the people or entities to whom those payments are due. Likewise, if you attempt to buy genuine love from a person, you will at some point find out that a person's presence can be bought but not their genuine love.

Bottom line: Money cannot buy love, and love can't physically pay bills.

The key principle of understanding that "money is only important where it works, and very unimportant where it does not" is essential to understanding true financial freedom. It gives you clarity regarding when and why money actually matters. Moreover, it keeps you from making the mistakes that many do with money in their attempt to use it in a manner for which it has no influence, and thus end up wasting their financial freedom. Understanding this concept will allow you to build financial freedom in a healthy and sustainable way. Moreover, it will keep you from becoming a slave to money or blind to the reality that even though money matters, it does not work as a panacea or a cure-all for every issue in life.

So, what is money?

Money is simply a *tool* that can be used to build, create, design, repair, restore, uplift, reform, or simplify. In the wrong hands, it can be a dangerous tool, but that does not mean money itself or having an abundance of it is evil. This is very important to understand. Many are often misguided in their pursuit of building wealth because of their lack of the fundamental understanding of it. Money itself is not evil or dangerous; however, *the love of money* is the root of all evil. Money is simply a tool you can use to create the life you want to live.

Why does money matter?

Money matters because it allows you to build and sustain the life of your choice. It matters because it allows you to create opportunities for yourself and others—to build, sustain, acquire, restore, and/or design what matters to you! Hopefully, what matters to you is positive for the society in which we all live.

Does money change you?

Despite popular sayings or beliefs, money itself does not change you. *Money magnifies who you already are.* It gives you the freedom to be more fulfilled in yourself, and as a result, people get to view the "real you." That "real you" appears to be a "changed you" because often the "real you" has been suppressed. If you are not forced to work so bills can be paid, and you can do more of what you truly want to do, the real you is free to be all that you can be. That doesn't mean the person you truly are can't change and/or become better. It just means that you alone *are* the change agent— not money, which is only a tool. The goal is to help you understand that money absolutely does not change you. Only you can change yourself.

Take some time to really think about what truly matters to you. That will be a driving force in helping you build wealth and possessing it in abundance properly. It will also keep you out of the traps that often cause many to forfeit their wealth. They are tricked into believing money is evil, it changes them, or that abundance is a bad thing. According to 2 Corinthians 9:8, God has no issue with us having an abundance. Furthermore, he has given us the power to gain abundance. Matthew 6:33 shares that if we "seek first the kingdom of God and His righteousness, all these things shall be added to [us]."

In summary keep the following mentally close:

1. Money matters because it is a tool you can use to do more of that which matters to you and the world around you—whatever that is! Hopefully, it will be a positive contribution to the world in which we all live.
2. Our perception is our reality. If we don't understand why money matters, we are at the mercy of everyone else's perceptions of why or if it matters. This leads to misguided actions and subsequent bad financial habits. Remember that money is very important where it works and very unimportant where it does not. Money by itself is not evil. Money cannot change you, but you can change yourself.
3. Understanding why money is important is vital. If you don't, you will either abuse it or it will abuse you. Don't let it define you. You define yourself.

Chapter 3

It's Simple, But Not Easy

When you find yourself in a hole, the first step in
getting out is to stop digging.
— Joel Gregory

The brilliance and simplicity found in wisdom never ceases to amaze us. When we stop and really take in the wisdom found in the quote that introduces this chapter, it is breathtaking how simply brilliant Joel Gregory makes it to pull ourselves out of any situation in life. Just stop digging. So simple, right?

Though it is simple, it is not easy! There is a difference between simple and easy, so please do not confuse the two. Simple can be defined as the "opposite of complicated." Simple can also be defined as "easily or readily understood." However, what the word "simple" does not mean is that it is easy to implement. Discipline, consistency, and the vigor required to build success is involved in that which is simple to understand.

If this sounds like I am trying to trick you, by no means is that the case. My goal is rather to ensure that you have all the tools to successfully navigate your way to growing and sustaining real financial freedom. In order to do so, you have to know it is simple, but not easy. If you are going to build and sustain financial freedom, it is essential for you to know that even though the blueprint or strategy is simple, putting it into practice is not easy.

If you want to succeed, please believe and know with everything in you that you absolutely can! No matter what the odds, anything is possible for you. The well-known motivational speaker Les Brown once said that "there are winners, there are losers, and there are those who have not discovered how to win yet!"

You must recognize that if you are going to build and sustain financial freedom, you have to take what is simple and plow through the difficult part of doing it every single day. Eric Thomas once said, "Everyone wants to be a beast (or winner), until it's time to do what beasts do!"

This is true of so many goals we want to achieve. We know what needs to be done. The strategy part is almost laughably simple, but the execution of it is not easy. It is the execution phase that is often the graveyard of good intentions. Getting up day after day after day to repeatedly do something requires incredible self-discipline and focus.

> *"Everyone wants to be a beast (or winner), until it's time to do what beasts do."* –Eric Thomas

In this chapter we will explore how you can win by recognizing some of the not so easy actions you must perform with methodical focus, discipline, consistency, and tenacity. Being real with yourself and recognizing when you are digging yourself into a financial hole or have fallen into one is vital. You need to understand how to stop digging and get out. Practical methods for developing positive habits for a healthy mindset will keep you from digging financial holes and thereby help you to sustain financial freedom.

So many things in our life fall under this category of "simple but not easy." It's simple to fall in love but not easy to stay in love.

It's simple to save money but not easy to stop spending money. It's simple to lose weight but not easy to eat right. It's simple to get married but not easy to stay happily married. It's simple to invest your money but not easy to get a return on your money. It's simple to start doing just about anything, but it's not easy to keep doing it.

Longevity is the litmus test for real success. Can you do what you need to do in order to be financially free and keep doing it for long periods of time? The answer is absolutely yes. However, finding those shovels you use to keep digging yourself into trouble and then eliminating them are key. After you locate and remove these particular hindrances in your life, then you must create the mental habits that help create abundance of wealth.

Let's be simple and clear. If you are struggling financially and just can't seem to get ahead, or perhaps you just simply want more money, usually only a handful of reasons exist for your current financial state. Perhaps you are making enough money to live, save, and grow, but you are spending more than you make. Maybe you are not making enough to live, save, and grow. No matter which category you fall into, the first step is to be real with yourself so you can stop digging.

Being real with ourselves is problematic for most of us. To honestly critique ourselves and build a blueprint to genuinely assist us in growing as individuals is hard. It takes the ability to swallow pride, be introspective in an unbiased manner, and then be sincere about it. We have to be able to examine ourselves honestly and keep ourselves accountable in order to succeed. To keep it real with ourselves is pretty simple. How? *We must stop lying to ourselves and be completely honest with ourselves.*

If you are looking for a deep physiological approach or politically correct one, sorry, but it's not here. If you are for real and want real success, you have to stop telling yourself lies! There are a few ways you can tell that you're lying to yourself: You talk about wanting more, yet you are doing nothing but talking about it. Or, you usually get up in the morning just in time to get to work and go to sleep with just enough time to do it again the next day. You sleep in on the weekends consistently. You watch television during the few hours between your working and sleeping hours. You spend little to no time educating yourself unless you're forced to do so.

You can't have what everyone else does not have by doing what everyone else is doing. It's time to get real. Do more! Work harder! Stop watching the lives of everyone else and focus on yours. Looking at television, Instagram, Facebook, and news outlets are major distractions and holes you are digging. You have to work on building yourself. The first step is to stop telling yourself you want more if you're not willing to put in more than the average person. If your actions don't add up to your talk, you are probably not being honest with yourself.

Stop telling yourself words that are not true about your financial situation. Believing and then saying to yourself that it will get better is good, but not being honest about where you are does not help you in the least. You must be cold and ruthless about where you are and where you want to be. Ask yourself these questions: What's my real net worth? How much debt do I really have? How much do I really make (after taxes and living expenses)? What can I truly afford? How much am I really saving? How can I save more?

In the next chapter, we will go into more detail about financial terms. If you are not real with yourself here, no real way exists for you to build and sustain financial success. You're living behind a façade that has to come to the light of truth at some point. So, you must build a real life instead.

Next, you need to recognize those specific things that are causing the setbacks. What holes do you keep digging in your finances? You could be digging yourself into a hole despite all of your great intentions, unaware that you are hurting yourself. The following list suggests ways you could be digging into a hole and don't realize it. How are you not being honest with yourself?

- You don't have a budget.
- You don't keep up with your budget honestly and consistently.
- You don't know your real net worth.
- You don't know/understand basic financial terms.
- You are programmed to impress others. You buy stuff you don't need and can't afford to impress others, as well as pay for others to impress them.
- You have no personal accountability, and you feel everything's always someone else's fault. But every time you blame something external for your financial woes, you give up power and dig your hole deeper.
- The original cost of your clothing, shoes, and purse exceeds your checking account balance.
- You are undisciplined and have no focus.
- You have too much pride.
- You take care of too many financial obligations that are not yours.

- You go to nightclubs or lounges but can't afford gas for your car.
- You are spending more than you make.
- You watch others too much (TV, Instagram, YouTube, Snapchat, Facebook, etc.) and are not doing anything to build your own life.
- You don't take care of your health, and your body reflects that. You eat too much and don't exercise, so you become tired and lazy with no energy to improve yourself.
- You tell yourself every day or week when you spend too much money that it's just for this day or week.
- You have a "you only live once" (YOLO) approach to your money. So, you spend, spend, spend and then have to work, work, work—never getting ahead.
- You try to keep up with friends and family.
- You buy new cars or more of a car than you need.
- You finance most large purchases—and even small ones.
- You keep running up credit card debt.
- You have no savings, but you still keep spending.
- You thrive on compliments and others' approval and spend money to get them.
- You eat out too much.
- You take too many days off.
- You waste time. Your focus is getting to Friday, instead of building wealth every day. When you get to Friday, you dig financial holes all weekend and are forced to go through another week trying to pay for the last weekend.
- You are scared of the truth.
- You are easily persuaded to spend.

- You are chasing every "get-rich quick" scheme. You can't do everything!
- You don't educate yourself.
- You can't say no.

This list can go on forever. If your hole is not on the list, you are responsible for being honest enough to recognize it and stop doing it. Nothing on this list is sustainable. Are these listed items more important than building and sustaining financial freedom in the bank? No, they're not! You have to decide that what you want matters more than pretending you don't have a problem. *You have to stop digging!*

After taking a look at this list, you realize how you have been digging some financial holes. You are being honest with yourself and have made the decision to get out of your holes and grow. Exercising discipline is required to obtain financial freedom but is not easy to consistently maintain. The strategy is simple, but acting in a methodically focused, disciplined, consistent, and determined manner is what separates those who succeed from those who do not.

Now that you have the knowledge to stop digging, you need a few practical methods and habit-forming practices to keep you out of the holes and start growing. As has been stated so many times before, this is a fairly simple concept to grasp. Develop a daily practice of reminding yourself what your financial goals are and why they supersede all the holes you were digging. You must have a daily reminder to strengthen your resolve to stop doing what is not helping and keep pushing toward your goal.

Each morning remind yourself out loud that you can and will become financially free, and then practice visualizing the life of financial freedom. Go over your "stop doing" list and keep it with you. Know your financial goals and daily budget and stick to them every day. Only give yourself access to that which you need. If you know you will be tempted, make it hard to spend by only taking the cash with you that you'll need. Don't carry cards. In the next few chapters, we will explore in more detail the principles of maintaining healthy finances and building financial goals.

In summary, keep in mind the following:

1. Building and sustaining financial freedom is simple but not easy to implement or do every day with consistency. Nevertheless, you are more than capable of doing it!
2. To do so, you must be real with yourself by identifying those behaviors that cause holes in your financial life and then stop doing them.
3. Be focused, disciplined, consistent, methodical, and determined in implementing the positive habits required for building success.
4. Whether you feel like it or not, work on your finances daily and make no excuse for just getting what is required done each day.

Chapter 4

Money Basics

An investment in knowledge
pays the best interest.
— Benjamin Franklin

Two of the most powerful statements I have ever read come from the writings of John Henrik Clarke, a historian and professor in the early 1900s, and Fredrick Douglass, the abolitionist. Clarke says, "Powerful people cannot afford to educate the people they oppress because once you are truly educated, you will not ask for power; you will take it." Douglass says, "Knowledge makes a man unfit to be a slave."

Please take a moment to let those statements soak into your mind. Essentially John H. Clarke and Fredrick Douglass are observing that true power lies in educating oneself. It is never given, but it is always assumed. Clarke is suggesting that those who have power know they will lose those they oppress if they truly educate them. They realize that if those who are oppressed ever get truly educated, they will no longer ask for power; instead, they will take it. They will then understand that they alone have the power to create the life they wish for and thus do not need to ask for it from another.

This concept is incredible in so many ways. For one, it reveals a secret that many people and organizations don't really wish you to know. Educating yourself is not just about sitting in a classroom flipping through textbooks, passing standardized tests, or blindly being told what the best way to accomplish goals is. It's not about your GPA or school name. *It's about assuming what you need in order to literally bend reality to your will.*

This mindset allows you to gain what is needed to create and build the life you want without asking for it. It is important to understand that truly educating yourself is not about having degrees or titles. It does not involve the mainstream ideology of education. It's about assuming the power you need through education to achieve your dreams. Gaining knowledge or education means obtaining practical worth and usefulness in service of something. You must know what that "in service of something" is for you. Why are you trying to educate yourself? In this process of educating yourself, you can't just sit and wait or ask nicely. You must insist, grind, and break through where doors are closed to acquire the education you need to succeed. Education truly is about empowering yourself!

> *I live life to be the ruler of my life—not a slave—to meet life as a powerful conqueror. Nothing exterior to me will ever take command of me.* – Walt Whitman

If you are going to live this kind of life by these words, you will have to become capable of something more powerful today than you were yesterday. The only way to do that is by educating yourself! Don't get trapped in others' definitions or in the stereotype of what education is. Understand that you can learn from everyone and almost anything. Don't be close-minded by limiting your reading to one author or so-called industry expert. Read them all and then conclude what's best for your own life.

Because we know the power of educating ourselves, let's begin by learning some financial basics. In this chapter we will explore the basics we need to start building upon to create and sustain financial freedom. We will define some key financial terms and elaborate on them for a clearer understanding. We will dive deeper into the significance of three specific terms (net worth, budget and financing) so we can truly understand the basics of building and sustaining financial freedom.

Let's start by defining key financial terms:

- **Cash** – money or currency in the form of coins or bank notes issued by a government. It is legal tender that can be used to exchange goods, debts, or services. Cash can also be money on hand or in a bank account, and/or marketable securities.

- **Marketable securities** – financial instruments that can be easily converted to cash, such as government bonds, common stock, or certificates of deposit. It can also involve debts that can be sold or redeemed within a year.
- **Liquidity** – the availability of cash or cash equivalents to meet short-term cash needs. In other words, liquidity is the amount of liquid assets that are available to pay expenses and debts as they become due. The most liquid asset of all is cash. This term describes the ease by which an asset can be converted into cash. It generally measures how much actual cash or cash equivalents you have available.
- **Asset** – any resource of value that can be converted into cash or a cash equivalent. An easy way to understand this is to consider an asset as anything that creates cash or a cash equivalent even while you are sleeping or not physical working for it directly. Cash that is in an account earning interest, real estate property with a positive cash flow, or a business with positive cash flow that runs with or without you are good examples of real assets.
- **Liabilities** – the amounts you owe to creditors or the people and organizations that lend you money. Typical liabilities include your mortgage, car payment, educational loans, personal loans, and credit card debt.
- **Debt** – an amount of money owed by a person, firm, or government (the borrower) to a lender. Debts arise when individuals, firms, or governments spend more than their current income or deliberately plan to borrow money to purchase specific goods, services, or assets.

- **Net worth** – Net worth is defined as assets minus liabilities (Net Worth = Assets - Liabilities). Essentially, it is a measure of how much a person or entity is truly worth financially.
- **Budget** – a financial plan for a defined period.
- **Financing** – asking any financial institution (bank, credit union, or finance company) or another person to lend you money that you promise to repay at some point in the future.
- **Credit** – money or its equivalent extended by a creditor, also known as a lender, to a debtor, also known as a borrower, for a mutually agreed upon set of terms and interest to be paid when money is paid back.
- **Interest** – payment from a borrower or deposit-taking financial institution to a lender or depositor of an amount above repayment of the principal sum (that is, the amount borrowed or deposited) at a particular rate. It is distinct from a fee that the borrower may pay the lender or some third party.
- **Compound interest** – interest you earn on interest. For example, using basic math, if you have a hundred dollars and it earns 5 percent interest each year, you will have $105 at the end of the first year. At the end of the second year, you'll have $110.25. Not only did you earn five dollars on the initial hundred-dollar deposit, but you also earned a quarter on the five dollars in interest. While a quarter may not sound like much at first, it adds up over time. Even if you never add another dime to that account, in ten years you'll have more than $162, thanks to the power of

compound interest, and in twenty-five years you'll have almost $340.

- **Interest rate** – the proportion of an amount loaned a lender charges as interest to the borrower, normally expressed as an annual percentage. It's the rate on the amount you pay in addition to what you borrowed.

What is true financial freedom? One of the most misunderstood fundamental concepts in personal finance concerns true financial freedom. Financial worth is not measured by your income or what you make. There are plenty of people who make lots of money and are still not financially free. As a matter of fact, they are dead broke. Financial worth is measured by what you actually have, or what you are actually worth. You can easily measure your actual financial worth by calculating your net worth. Remember that your **Net Worth = Your Assets - Your Liabilities/Debts**. It is important to know that net worth has nothing to do with your salary or annual income. There are plenty of financially free people with small salaries or minimal annual incomes. The key is the amount of money you make that you actually keep and maintain on a consistent basis.

For an illustration, let's calculate two fictitious individuals' net worth.

Mr. A's income or annual salary:

> – $120,000 per year

Mr. A's assets:

> – $1,200 – Savings
> – $300 – Checking account
> – $30,0000 – Car value

> **Total assets = $31,500**

Mr. A's liabilities:

> – $35,000 – Car note
> – $15,000 – Apartment rental lease for a year
> – $50,000 – Credit card debt
> – $25,000 – Student loan debt

> **Total liabilities or debt = $125,000**

Mr. A's net worth is actually negative:

$31,500 (assets) - 125,000 (liabilities) = ($93,500) (net worth)

Miss. B's income or annual salary:

    – $60,000 per year

Miss. B's assets:

    – $40,000 – Savings
    – $3,000 – Checking account
    – $7,000 – Car value
    – $250,000 – Home property value

                Total Assets = $300,000

Miss. B's liabilities:

    – $0 –   Car debt
    – $0 –   Credit card debt
    – $0 –   Student loan debt
    – $100,000 – Mortgage/loan on home

                Total liabilities or debt = $100,000

Miss. B's net worth is **$300,000 (assets) - $100,000 (liabilities) = $200,000 (net worth)**

    Regarding these two examples of net worth calculations, you can learn several basic money lessons. One is that your income does not factor into your net worth, even though it can help you grow your net worth. Don't be confused about this: it is not what you make but what you keep that matters. People love to tout their salaries and what they make. Mr. A makes twice as much money as Miss. B. However, Mr. A has no net worth. (He's essentially broke and forced to keep working.) Mr. A owes more than he has in actual assets, which means he has no real wealth.

Miss. B, despite the fact that she makes much less money, is actually wealthier than Mr. B. Moreover, Miss. B has the financial freedom and flexibility to take risks. She is not forced to work. It is crucial to understand that your financial health is not measured by social standards but rather on actual numbers. Numbers are non-biased. Your car, house, and clothes absolutely do not determine your financial worth. A person without financial freedom can still drive a very nice car, own a very nice home, and wear very nice clothes. Yet that does not mean they are financially successful or free. When building and sustaining your wealth, you must know what real financial freedom is and what it is not. In simple terms, *real financial freedom originates with positive net worth.*

Now that you understand some of the basics of net worth, you must learn how to develop it. How do you keep more of what you earn? It's simple, but not easy, as we have learned. Start by spending less than you make, and do it consistently. How do you that? By minimizing (decreasing as much as possible) your spending and maximizing (growing) your income. In order to do so, you absolutely must have a budget or spending plan. There's no way around it! Remember that a budget is simply a financial plan for a defined period of time. It helps you monitor and control your expenses, as well as your income. A budget will help you consistently keep more of what you earn. It is harder to spend when you have a plan by which you keep track of expenditures every day. This chapter only focuses on a few basic terms. We will go into additional detail regarding some practical ways to build and sustain your budget or spending plan in the next chapter.

The final term that we will concentrate on in this chapter is financing. Remember, financing means asking any financial institution (bank, credit union, or finance company) or another person to lend you money that you promise to repay at some point in the future.

When you take out a loan to buy something, your lender purchases that item for you and allows you to pay it back over an agreed period of time. Essentially, the lender provides you the service of using its money, and in exchange, you compensate the lender for its services by paying interest.

Simply stated, financing is borrowing from your future self, and then paying another for the opportunity to do so. Proverbs 22:7 (NIV) states, "A borrower is a slave to the lender."

Many people don't understand what takes place when they are financing items. You are not paying the actual face value or sales price plus applicable taxes for that item. You end up paying much more because whomever you borrow from will typically charge interest on what they lend you. For example, if you take out a twenty thousand-dollar car loan at 5 percent and you borrow the money over four years, your monthly payment will be approximately $460.59 (not including dealer fees or any extras you purchase), assuming you pay the sales tax of 7 percent or $1,400 in cash up front. At the end of four years, you'll have paid $2,108.12 in interest, in addition to paying back the original twenty thousand. In effect, you would pay $20,000 + $1,400 + $2,108.12 = $23,508.12. You would have saved

$2,108.12 if you had not financed the car. You could have saved all this money by paying in cash.

If you can avoid financing, please do! You will be able to keep so much more of your earnings. Financing is sometimes required. However, it is wise not to finance any item that will not grow in value after purchase or does not directly assist in generating earnings for you. Financing should be used as a tool to help you generate more earnings you can keep. Don't allow the allure of being able to purchase something now overrule the reality of whether not that item is truly needed. Does that new item truly help you build and sustain your financial freedom?

In summary, review the key money terms. Spend time making sure that you truly understand them and their practical application in your personal finances. Remember, your net worth is not what you earn but what you actually have. Calculate your personal net worth and start tracking its growth. A budget is an absolute must to consistently manage your money. Only finance items if they grow in value after your purchase or directly assist you in generating earnings. Put your understanding of the money basics to work for you!

Chapter 5

Flight Plan

Victory awaits him who has
everything in order.
—Roald Amundsen

Born in 1872, Norwegian Roald Amundsen decided by the age of fifteen that he wanted to have a career as an explorer. During the late 1880s, he joined several Arctic expeditions, including the first one to survive the Arctic winter. After serving as a mate on an Antarctic expedition, at the age of twenty-five he began to plan his own expedition. His goals were to navigate the Northwest Passage, which linked the Atlantic to the Pacific, and become the first person to reach the South Pole. Amundsen was not alone in his desire or attempt to be the first man to reach the South Pole. Captain Robert Falcon Scott, an explorer and officer in the British Royal Navy, was also endeavoring to accomplish this daring task.

In preparation for this seemingly impossible quest, Amundsen learned about survival in extremely cold places by living with the Eskimos. He learned about wearing animal skins instead of heavy furs. He also studied sailing techniques, steam navigation, scientific navigation, and terrestrial magnetism, as well as trained himself to endure bitter cold and long travel.

Amundsen planned his voyage with meticulous clarity and carried it out with tenacious discipline, despite the harsh rigors involved and low chances of succeeding. During his journey

Amundsen planned that each day he would only go twenty miles. Even on great days when the weather was perfect for traveling, he only traveled twenty miles. With consistent discipline Amundsen went this distance each day toward his goal. Captain Scott, on the other hand, was inconsistent in his daily approach. He would only travel five to ten miles or not go at all on bad days, and forge ahead for twenty to twenty-five miles on good days.

Enduring the unforgiving terrain and the brutally cold winter, Amundsen reached the South Pole on December 14, 1911, ahead of the expedition led by Captain Scott. How? What led to this incredible success in one of the most brutally cold and frozen places on earth? It's simple. Amundsen had a clear plan and executed it with fanatical discipline.

Likewise, your monetary success requires a plan to develop financial freedom and then sustain it. Like Amundsen, we not only need a plan, but we also need to execute it with fanatical discipline and consistency despite the rugged terrain of life that makes it difficult. It is important to understand that anyone who intends to succeed must have definite plans. In this chapter we will explore basics of what a financial plan looks like and how to be disciplined in executing that plan.

A financial plan must comprise several key components:

- **A goal**
    - o   Where do you want to be? Where are you going?

- **A solid framework**
    - o   Fanatical discipline for every dollar you earn

- **A budget**
    - o   Benchmark and visual guide

- **A tenacious and relentless execution**
    - o   No excuses and full accountability

Let us explore each component. Your financial goal should be simple and clear. Not much science is involved for this one at all. Where are you headed? How financially successful do you want to be? What is that special number for you? Think about the life you want to live without the stress or concern of having to work every day to afford it. What do you want to be able to do every day? What makes up your drive to meet your goal? Would you be driven? Where do you want to live—in a nice small home on the beach, or in the countryside? Who do you want to help? God has a plan for your prosperity. What do you envision regarding the Lord's plans for your life? Line up the plan for your life according to God's plan for your destiny.

Stop for a moment and sincerely visualize the best life for you. Now write down the ideal amount of money you'll need to enjoy that lifestyle and place the note somewhere you can see it every day. To ensure you have the right number, reach out to a financial adviser or your local banker and let them help you. Ask them how much money they believe you will need to retire in the way you desire. Just make sure you build that number based on what you truly want and understand the reason why. Accomplishing a goal is hard if you don't truly know your motivation. It is important to write down your dreams and know why. Your why will drive you when it becomes difficult to stay disciplined during the execution phase. Your why is *your* why. It doesn't have to make sense to anyone else because the reason is yours alone!

The financial framework will be the foundation of your plan to help you stay focused. It involves what you do with every single dollar that you earn. The following is a solid financial framework:

- **For every dollar earned, you should attempt to allocate it as shown (after taxes are taken out).**
  - ○ **55 cents or 55 percent** is allocated for living expenses (food, rent, mortgage, car, phone, healthcare, etc.).
  - ○ **25 cents or 25 percent** is allocated for savings.
  - ○ **10 cents or 10 percent** is allocated for charity or gifts.
  - ○ **10 cents or 10 percent** is allocated for investing in growing yourself. and/or growing your net worth (investing and educating yourself).

This does not mean that you can't increase your savings or decrease your expenses. This should only be a basic framework in which you build your financial plan. Take your income after taxes are taken out and then apply the percentages found in this financial framework illustration. This keeps you moving in the right direction and ensures that you keep growing.

Now let's take a look at the spending plan. Your budget should include all of your income, savings, and expenses. It should give you a clear picture of what you plan to earn, save, and spend. The following is an example of a personal budget:

Monthly Budget Template

Income for the month of _____

Item	Amount
Salary	
Spouse's salary	
Dividends	
Interest	
Investments	
Reimbursements	
Other	
Total:	

Expenses for the month of _____

Item	Amount
Mortgage/rent	
Car loan	
Car insurance	
House insurance	
Life insurance	
Childcare	
Charity	
Gas/electricity	
Telephone	
Cable	
Internet	
Food	
Gas for car	
Pet supplies	
Healthcare	
Entertainment	
Gifts	
Clothing	
Other	
Total:	

Income vs. expenses:

Item	Amount
Monthly income	
Monthly expenses	
Difference:	

This sample spending plan template can be used to prioritize your spending and keep you on target. Once your goal has been set, your solid framework can be put in place and your budget accurately and honestly designed. Now you must begin to take the journey of staying disciplined in executing your plan. Don't spend more than your spending plan dictates. Pay attention to every dollar you spend. Don't finance things you can't afford, especially items that don't help you earn more. Don't waste your time and energy on things that do not help you reach your goal. Chapters 1, 2, and 3 really come to life here. You have to remember what the holding patterns of your life are and resolve not to repeat them. Remember why money is important and remind yourself it is simple, but not easy. We must view ourselves as managers of God's resources to make sure that we pay attention to every dollar spent.

There are no excuses. A wise man once told me that "excuses are the cousin to a lie wrapped in the skin of a reason." Excuses build bridges to nowhere and monuments to nothing. If you are fanatically disciplined in your execution of the plan and give yourself no excuses, you will obtain financial freedom! Make the plan today and see to it that it has a goal, a solid framework, and a spending regimen. Then, stay tenacious and relentless in its implementation.

Chapter 6

It's a Marathon, Not a Sprint

*Learn to live a lifestyle you can maintain
for a lifetime.*
—Steven W. Zachary II

Everyone wants financial success now. According to the North American Association of State and Provincial Lotteries, in 2016 Americans spent a total of $73.5 billion on traditional lottery tickets, despite the reality that statistically they are more likely to be eaten by a shark or struck by lightning before they'd ever win the lottery. Even if by a stroke of luck they do win, according to the National Endowment for Financial Education (NEFE), 70 percent of lottery winners end up bankrupt in just a few years after receiving a large financial windfall. Without an understanding and consistent practice of successful financial sustaining principles, they won't sustain their financial freedom, even if they win the lottery.

So, how do you sustain wealth? You begin by understanding what the word "sustain" actually means. The Cambridge Dictionary defines it this way: "to cause or allow something to continue for a period of time." You want to ensure that you are building financial freedom in a sustainable manner.

> *Sustainability: a method of using (not hoarding) resources so that they are not depleted or permanently damaged. To sustain your financial freedom, you must first learn how to use resources without damaging or depleting them.* –Tim White

Professional athletes are often paid in a manner that is not sustainable for their lifetime but rather for a short period of time, especially if the athlete is spending at or above their actual income level. There is no lifetime longevity for a professional athlete. The average career span, according to Statista, for a professional NHL player is about 5.5 years, a professional basketball player 4.5 years and 3.5 years for an NFL player. Their salary doesn't last a lifetime or anywhere close.

Many athletes go broke after their career because they live a lifestyle according to the amount of money they used to make while playing their sport. Once they are no longer playing and earning money at that rate, it is difficult for them to adjust their lifestyle of flagrant spending. This is why you must *learn to live a lifestyle you can maintain for a lifetime.*

To truly sustain your financial freedom, you must live beneath your means for a lifetime. Another way to explain this is by the example of fad diets. People can push really hard for sixty to ninety days and lose a lot of weight. However, their effort is often not sustainable because they have not changed their entire lifestyle to maintain the weight loss or muscles built. They don't eat to live, so they fall back into living to eat. They don't eat so they can run/work out; instead, they run/work out so they can eat.

Many of us are guilty of this. We don't alter the way we think about food, what we eat, or how much we eat. Nevertheless, eating a healthy diet can't be a ninety-day test but a crucial part of our lifestyle that becomes automatic for us. The same is true for the way we build and spend our income. It has to be a lifestyle we've not only built for us to enjoy but also one that can sustain us for our lifetime.

I know you are thinking, *That sounds great, but how?*

1. Make the financial framework and basics a lifestyle and add to it. Form regular habits that include sticking to your spending plan and focusing on growing your net worth. Build your spending decisions around your goals rather than living like a superstar. Now, you can still enjoy your life while you do this, but you just have to plan for things you enjoy. In some cases, you need to be patient enough to earn and save first. If all you enjoy cannot immediately go in the spending plan, be disciplined and patient: it's coming. It's about relative frugality, which is the cornerstone of personal finance. You don't have to be ridiculously frugal, but you do have to be honest and disciplined based on your situation.

2. Take your financial framework and double down on it. If you are making more than it takes you to live, double down or clamp down as hard as you can on your savings, investments, mortgage or debt retirement. Allow compound interest to work in your favor. Remember, your financial framework is designed to make sure every dollar you earn is allocated in a manner that builds your financial freedom (55 percent for living expenses, 25 percent for savings, 10 percent for charity/gifts, and 10 percent for self-investment [based on after tax dollars]). If you can live on less and save and invest more of your money, do it now.

When you receive lump sums of cash, save it rather than spending it. This allows you to build your assets and allow them to work for you, ultimately building enough reserves to maintain your life without any additional effort from you. Your cash on hand pays you interest that is compounding annually. Your investments build more cash flow, and that cash provides additional interest earnings. You want to turn your earnings/income, savings, and investments into high-income producing assets, which means that they create income by themselves for you.

3. Don't get in a hurry. A vital key to building and sustaining real financial freedom is to not get in a hurry. It takes time.

> **Saving only $100 per month from age 25 to age 65 at 12% growth = $1,176,000. Everyone should retire a millionaire!**
> —Dave Ramsey, February 12, 2013

Enjoy the process of building. I once heard comedian Jim Carrey say he wished everyone could truly experience great wealth so they could realize having it is not as great as they sometimes believe. The process and the journey, the people with whom you build relationships, and the excitement of learning as well as accomplishing new goals are truly a rewarding part of the voyage. Enjoy it!

People in a hurry look for shortcuts, but there are none for achieving financial success. In fact, success is not a sprint, but a marathon. Even if you start the race ahead of the pack, a long process still lies ahead to build and sustain your wealth.

Poker is one of the most complex games in the world, requiring an abnormal amount of patience and focus. Many argue it is much more complex than chess because there are so many ever-changing variables, including possible card variations and opponents. The best two cards you can be dealt at the start of a No Limit Hold 'em poker game is two aces (aka pocket aces). The probability you will be dealt these two cards together is 6/1326, or statistically once every 221 hands dealt. That's a very slim chance! According to poker statistics, the probability of winning with pocket aces at the start of a hand is 31.36%, assuming all players stay in until the end. However, that is a big if. You are still not guaranteed to win. There is still almost a 70 percent chance you'll lose, even though you may have the best starting hand in the game.

The point is simple: the best hand does not always win. So, regarding your money, if by chance you were dealt an amazing starting hand, or a horrible one but you found a shortcut that may provide you with an amazing hand, you could still end up losing if you don't practice the principles of building and sustaining your financial freedom. Applying the skills you've learned with the consistency necessary to maintain success in life and finances to the end, despite the hand dealt, is crucial.

For those of you waiting to win the lottery or a poker game with pocket aces, I have good and bad news. The bad news is that success is never accidental, and the good news is that success is never accidental. Phil Jackson once said that "there is no such thing as an unintentional championship." Intentionality and strategy must be a given for you to ultimately enjoy victory!

Usually, one big score doesn't happen. In fact, there is a very low percentage chance of that. Bottom line: Don't wait on the lottery or a big windfall. If that does happen, great! But you still need to know and consistently use the tools for building and keeping financial freedom even if you hit big. Please understand the odds are not in your favor if you are looking to hit a huge score.

Even entrepreneurs who sell their companies for huge sums did not hit it big overnight. They work tremendously hard (in most cases for seven to fifteen years) before being in a place to sell for a substantial amount. A study by MIT found that the average age of start-up founders is around forty-two, and the average age of entrepreneurs who founded high-growth companies is forty-five. The study also found that twenty-something founders have the lowest likelihood of starting a company with a successful exit.

In summary, building and sustaining financial freedom truly is a marathon, not a sprint. Learn to live a lifestyle you can maintain for a lifetime by staying disciplined through the consistent application of financial principles.

1. Understand what it means to sustain your financial freedom. Remember that sustainability is a method of using (not hoarding) a resource so that the resource is not depleted or permanently damaged.
2. Make your financial framework a lifestyle, not a diet. By making it a regular habit, you'll ensure that it gets implemented automatically. Every dollar you earn will be shifted into the right place without any extra thought.
3. Don't get in a hurry. It does not matter what your hand is in life; success is never accidental. It takes work, and there are no shortcuts.

Chapter 7

Give More Than You Take

Laugh more than you cry, love more than you hate,
and give more than you take.
—Dr. Shawn E. E. Thomas

What you hold back from life, life holds back from you. What you give to life, life gives to you. Most people who are struggling financially have not truly learned the art of giving—not just giving monetarily, but truly giving of themselves. When you truly learn to give without the expectation of something in return, you attract amazing people and benefits who will create a sustainable abundance in your life.

A wise man once said, "You give so little when you give of your possessions. It is when you give of yourself that you truly give." Learning how to genuinely and selflessly give encouragement, love, time, wisdom, energy, and money is crucial to building and sustaining wealth. I once heard my childhood pastor, Clarence Warren, say, "There are those who give little of the much they have, and they give it for recognition. Then there are those who give without wanting any recognition." He would also often repeat this old saying, "Judge a man not by what he does, but what he does not have to give and yet still does. To judge the true quality of a person, ask yourself what he or she does when nobody's looking."

Giving is an art that should be practiced with consistency. When one gives, it creates abundance beyond belief. Why is giving so important? Our feelings of compassion, humanity, and a sense of appreciation awaken when we give to others. These generous behaviors are contagious. If people see you or others giving back to society in some shape or form, it is likely they will be inspired to reciprocate. Many people who give back to society have been motivated by someone in their community or environment who has already done so.

People want to be around, buy from, work with, do business with, and help people they like. When you learn to give of yourself, you will see your life flourish beyond belief because the act of giving attracts other amazing people. Giving your time, money, kindness, support, knowledge, and encouragement, yet expecting nothing in return is key. It creates a world in which what you give is given back to you, even though you may have more than you could ever need.

Many people give just enough at work to get the job done. But then they are upset when they receive either a little raise or none at all—and definitely no promotion. But why should they get one? They are giving the bare minimum yet expect more in return. People who learn to go beyond eventually receive beyond, even if in the midst of it all they are hurt or taken advantage of. They make giving a lifestyle, not a condition.

Giving is typically a character trait in people who understand that it is better to give than receive. I know this sounds counterproductive in the financial world. But when you learn to work harder than the job demands, you position yourself to get a better job or become self-employed. When you do more work than the job pays, you eventually end up with more pay. When you work for almost free, as billionaire Warren Buffet once did to gain access to people and knowledge, what you give ends up giving back to you so much more than you could ever imagine.

Think about people you know who work harder than they are paid to do. These individuals are wired to always give more than they take. They find themselves surrounded by people who want to do more for them. In turn, they always have more opportunities and all the great things that create a wonderful life of abundance. Think about the people for whom you like to do favors. Usually, it's not the entitled or ungrateful. It's not those who think you owe them something. Instead, it's those who give to you without wanting or expecting anything in return. It's people who are grateful to offer their kindness, encouragement, love, support, time, effort, energy, and money.

Giving can also be the very source of your monetary abundance. In John Bunyan's 1684 classic *The Pilgrim's Progress*, Old Honest poses this riddle to the innkeeper Gaius: "A man there was, tho' some did count him mad; the more he cast away, the more he had." Gaius solves the riddle by stating, "He that bestows his Goods upon the Poor, shall have as much again, and ten times more."

The point of this riddle is that giving can fill you with abundance. To most people, this is counterintuitive. It is obvious that you must have money before you can give it away, right? Or in the words of former British prime minister Margaret Thatcher, "No one would remember the Good Samaritan if he'd only had good intentions—he had money too."

At any rate, Bunyan's Gaius was right, and economic research backs him up. Statistics from real data support the principle that giving stimulates prosperity, for both individuals and nations. Charity apparently can help you create financial freedom.

> *"We cannot predict the future, but we can create it!"* –Jim Collins

The United States is a remarkably charitable nation. The Giving U.S.A. Foundation estimates that Americans donated nearly $410 billion to charity in 2018. This is more than the gross domestic product (the annualized value of goods and services produced within a nation) of all but thirty-three countries in the world. More than three-quarters of these donations came from private individuals. Additional research suggests that between 65 and 85 percent of Americans give to charities each year.

How does all this giving relate to high levels of prosperity? The Social Capital Community Benchmark Survey is a survey of about thirty thousand people in more than forty communities across the U. S. It is one of the best single sources of data available regarding the civic participation of Americans. The S.C.C.B.S., which takes into account differences in education, age, race, religion, and other personal characteristics, shows that people who give charitably make significantly more money than those who don't. While that seems like common sense, it turns out that the link in the data between giving and earning is not just one-way. People do give more when they become richer—research has shown that a 10 percent increase in income stimulates giving by about 7 percent—but people also grow wealthier when they give more.

Giving encourages dialogue between people, communities, and nations in ways that they would not ordinarily have experienced previously. When people choose to give, they unite from different sectors and communities in the name of a common cause. This is a key contributing factor in strengthening communities and nation-building. We do not live our lives alone. Instead, it takes collaboration to achieve greatness. Practically everything we do or will do that is worth doing will require the help of someone giving. If you think about those you know who have massive amounts of wealth, they typically do a tremendous amount of giving.

How does God feel about giving?

He who has a generous eye will be blessed, for he gives of his bread to the poor.
(Proverbs 22:9)

He covets greedily all day long,
But the righteous gives and does not spare.
(Proverbs 21:26)

So let each one *give* as he purposes in his heart, not grudgingly or of necessity; for God loves a cheerful giver.
(2 Corinthians 9:7)

He who has pity on the poor lends to the LORD,
And He will pay back what he has given.
(Proverbs 19:17)

He who gives to the poor will not lack,
But he who hides his eyes will have many curses.
(Proverbs 28:27)

"I have shown you in every way, by laboring like this, that you must support the weak. And remember the words of the Lord Jesus, that He said, 'It is more blessed to give than to receive.'"
(Acts 20:35)

"Bring all the tithes into the storehouse, that there may be food in My house, and try me now in this, says the LORD of hosts, if I will not open for you the windows of heaven and pour out for you *such* blessing that *there will* not *be room* enough *to receive it.*"
(Malachi 3:10)

This book provides a simple blueprint that—if followed with rigorous consistency and tenacious discipline—you may obtain financial freedom. In summary, make sure you do the following:

1. Break the holding patterns that cause you to "run around in circles" financially.

2. Understand why money matters, and use that knowledge to work for you in building and sustaining wealth.

3. Don't forget that it is simple but not easy. Execution of your plan will take work, but it can be done if you stay focused.

4. Educate yourself on money basics and additional financial principles to help you grow and sustain your wealth. Know the key financial terms shared and how they are applicable to your financial life.

5. You must have a plan. It is vital to your success.

6. Remember that it's a marathon, not a sprint. Success is not accidental. Take your time.

7. Learn to give more than you take. Be the person who attracts and sustain abundance through giving more.

Author Jim Collins once stated, "We cannot predict the future, but we can create it!" Follow this blueprint and create financial freedom in your future.

www.ingramcontent.com/pod-product-compliance
Lightning Source LLC
Chambersburg PA
CBHW030843210326
41458CB00065B/6711/J

Thank you for reading!

For additional resources, please visit:

www.GetFinancialFreedomNow.com